Praise for *Hiring the Heavens*

"Accessing spiritual assistance for everyday life events — what a concept! Very often we don't think to ask for help unless confronted with a major problem or life-threatening situation. Jean breaks through all the preconceived notions about 'asking' and presents a clear, concise how-to book helping us to tap into and use the limitless powers that prevail on a daily basis. With this information, life becomes easier."

— Susan Bryant, author of
Beyond the B.S.: Belief System Restructuring

"I read the book in about an hour and started creating committees immediately. Several of my committees have done fantastic jobs and have made my life become more prosperous and flow easier. For example, I hired a real estate committee and had a new place to live with all of my specifications within five days, and marketing committees have brought me new business. The tasks are infinite, and the angelic beings are very happy because these duties help them to grow and evolve as well. Thank you, Jean, for bringing the book out to the public."

— Tiffany Cano, certified pranic healing instructor

Hiring the

heavens

Hiring the *heavens*

A Practical Guide
to Developing Working Relationships
with the Spirits of Creation

Jean Slatter

New World Library
Novato, California

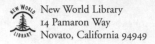 New World Library
14 Pamaron Way
Novato, California 94949

Originally published by Personal Transformation Press in 2003.

Design by Mary Ann Casler
Typography by Tona Pearce Myers

Library of Congress Cataloging-in-Publication Data
Slatter, Jean.
Hiring the heavens : a practical guide to developing working relationships with the spirits of Creation / Jean Slatter.
    p.   cm.
ISBN 1-57731-512-X (pbk. : alk. paper)
1. Angels. 2. Spirits. 3. Spiritual life. I. Title.
BL477.S56 2005
202'.15—dc22   2004026251

First New World Library edition, April 2005
ISBN 1-57731-512-X
ISBN-13 978-1-57731-512-4

Printed in Canada on acid-free, partially recycled paper

 New World Library is a proud member of the Green Press Initiative.

Distributed to the trade by Publishers Group West

20 19 18 17 16 15 14 13

contents

setting the Stage

I was guided to write this book. At first I couldn't imagine how my ideas could fill a book — they seemed too simple! After all, I had been using them for years without any special effort or training. They had become so much a part of my life that I never went through a day without them. It took as little as ten minutes to share my process with friends, so how could I possibly expand the material enough to create an entire book? Yet that's what my inner guidance insisted upon.

It began to dawn on me that the simplicity of my process was its greatest beauty. I loved the idea of offering a path to Spirit that seemed like child's play, one so easy and open-hearted that it left room for the reader's own imagination to flower. I wanted my book to be short and sweet, yet over-flowing with possibilities — something that could be read in a few hours and yet potentially change the reader's perceptions in a profound and lasting way.

I knew I would need to depict what I've come to call the Spirits of Creation in a way that would inspire rather than confine the reader. I decided to use various terms (celestial helpers, invisible assistants, cosmic forces, angels, guides, Spirit, the Heavens, the Divine, and so on) that could be interpreted as literally or symbolically as the reader wished. I knew that many people would view the Spirits of Creation as actual beings, while others might see them as facets of their own inner or higher selves or simply as a handy way to conceptualize the infinite resources and benevolence of the nonphysical dimension. Or all of the above! More than anything, I wanted my book to open a beautiful doorway that could be entered by readers with diverse backgrounds and perspectives.

So, in the spring of 2002, I began to put pen to paper. And I watched as my ideas, while retaining their precious simplicity, began to deepen and fill out. As the book evolved, my own personal awareness about who we really are and what we're here to do expanded dramatically.

Many spiritual teachers tell us that life is a gift to be lived in joyful alignment with our divine source. But until a few years ago I didn't understand that to achieve this alignment, I had to own, accept, and *employ* the part of me that is divine. Otherwise, my essence and my purpose in this lifetime would not be fully expressed.

Employ my own divinity? What exactly did that mean? I discovered that for me the answer lay at the heart of creating my own reality, a very popular idea these days but one that only became real for me when I embraced the employment concept described in this book. Ultimately, it meant a shift in perception that changed the way I viewed everything.

It all began when I came to understand that I was not alone, that spiritual helpers stood ready and willing to be hired in the cocreative expression of my divinity. Unified with Spirit, I realized I was master of my universe and designer of my world. This was a message of freedom and power.

I must admit that much of what I'm about to share came as a big surprise to me. Watching it unfold was an exhilarating experience, but it also triggered some internal resistance. Part of this revelation, I felt at first, bordered on irreverence. I now recognize that my apprehension was nothing more than growing pains within my consciousness. As my spirit expanded into fuller understanding, new perceptions replaced those beliefs that no longer served me.

When I shared this information with others, I received heartfelt responses from many people who also heard an inner whisper urging them to create their lives in tandem with the power of the Universe. I came to see myself as a bridge, and my mission as one of connecting people with the spiritual world in a tangible, easily embraceable way. Writing this book was an inevitable step on my path toward owning and accepting my own divine power — and inspiring others to do the same.

Hiring the *heavens*

Bringing Heaven Down to *earth*

Do you feel connected to Spirit? I'm not talking about whether or not you have a religious background or affiliation. I'm talking about being connected to the power of the Heavens — and bringing it right down here to Earth to use in your everyday life.

For many people, spiritual connection means going to church and praying. And even though they may believe they have a soul or spirit within, they feel separate from the power of the Universe. They can worship it and form religions around it, but it remains outside of them. Only in times of crisis or in service of a noble cause do they feel justified in calling upon that power — and even then they believe the response (or lack thereof) is entirely up to God.

Even those of us who believe in our oneness with Spirit often find it difficult to envision such a tremendous force as a tangible, viable energy in our daily lives. The idea that we're all part of God may be inspiring, but it's just pretty prose unless we can somehow get it into bite-sized pieces.

What we really need is a way to make our lives better, a way to be happier and more at ease — to find a fulfilling job, create a great marriage, help our kids, be a good friend, pay our bills, and reduce the stress in our lives. We all want to get through the day with as much grace and wisdom as possible.

We need help with the real stuff in life — the ups and downs and challenges and yearnings we experience every day. If the power of the Heavens can't be brought down to that level, then of what earthly use is it? I don't expect to be creating planets anytime soon, do you?

It's amazing, really. Many of us believe we are divine vessels in physical form, and yet, take any mundane human problem, such as a bill that needs to be paid or a deadline that's too close, and suddenly we forget all about that. We may believe we were born with the power that created the world, but we fall apart when we have to create a workable schedule! Somehow our true nature gets buried under the constant hum of our busy minds, our busy lives, and our busy fears. Despite all the poetic reassurance of the omnipotent support within us that's provided by popular religion these days, we still feel alone.

But what if it could be different? Let's explore a shift in perception that will make your connection to the creative force of the Heavens so real you can reach out and grasp it, one that will turn familiar but abstract expressions, such as "God is within you," and "Ask and you shall receive," into something immediate and real. Suddenly the expansive power of the Universe, which seemed so impossible to relate to, will be sitting right in the palm of your hand. God — and all of the Heavens — will become your ally and your confidant, sitting right beside you and supporting your every intention.

In these pages you'll discover a fresh, revitalized way of looking at spirituality that will ever so gently bring God down to Earth. And consider this: What if that's exactly where He's always wanted to be? What if He's been calling to you all along, reminding you that you are an extension of Him, and that as such it is your prerogative — no, your God-given mission — to take command of this omnipresent power? As far as I'm concerned, the most important message in my book is this: *by divine design we are creators, and it is our birthright — indeed, our directive — to joyfully wield the power of the Universe.*

This bears repeating: we are extensions of the creative energy of the Universe, and this vast resource is always available to us. The same creative force that existed from the beginning of time is our essential nature. Flowing through each of us is a dynamic energy that is ours to use deliberately to create the life we desire. Its potential is unlimited, unbounded — and it *belongs* to us all.

When we see ourselves as divinely sanctioned creators, something quite amazing happens. The transformation is unmistakable. We live life from a different vantage point. We recognize our authority to summon the vast resources of the Heavens and all of the eager spiritual assistance that's available for everything we do. We discover that all conceivable tasks can be facilitated and orchestrated and all conceivable problems can be solved by our connection to this incredible power. With this new awareness we can shape our lives purposefully, creating joy and fulfillment with such ease that it feels like a miracle. From now on our lives can be deliberate, joyful expressions of the infinite Source of all creation and possibilities. Heaven can finally be brought down to Earth.

It's really quite simple. It's as near as your next thought — or even closer. Even if you read no more than the first few chapters of this book, your life can be changed forever.

As Oliver Wendell Holmes said, "A mind stretched by a new idea can never go back to its original dimensions."

Are you ready to have your mind stretched?

CHAPTER 2

Hiring in the *spiritual* Realm

Just for fun, imagine that the spiritual world is every bit as diverse as our own physical world. Imagine that it possesses every personality, style, skill, interest, motivation, talent, and ability that we humans do. For example, here on Earth we find people with all kinds of personality traits. Some are funny, some are analytical, some are spontaneous or assertive or efficient. We also find people with every possible talent, ability, and job description. Some are exceptional as teachers, some as negotiators, some as gardeners or counselors or child-care providers.

Now imagine that all of these characteristics and job descriptions also exist in the nonphysical dimension, that every subject has a match in the spiritual realm. Science, mathematics, art, music, philosophy, construction, and every other possible arena all have their spiritual doubles. For a talent or ability to exist here on Earth, its corresponding nonphysical energy must also exist.

Next, imagine that this entire universe of celestial experts and attributes is yours for the asking. Imagine that the Spirits of Creation are standing ready to assist you in making your world. Believe that not only is the power to summon that creativity flowing through you, it is your divine right — divine *assignment,* even — to wield it.

I have seen that what I've just described is true. How could this reality change your life? What if all of these skills, traits, and talents were indeed at your fingertips?

The Universal Yellow Pages

Let's go even further and imagine that each of us has access to the expansive, unabridged, revised-every-minute Yellow Pages of the Universe. Next time you're in need of a special talent or skill, let your imagination do the walking! Whatever project or need you may have, I invite you to open the Universal Yellow Pages and choose the professionals with the perfect skills to assist you.

If a talent or ability exists here on Earth, the Universal Yellow Pages has a section for it. In fact, even if you've never heard of anyone with the exact package of skills and traits you're looking for, you can be confident that somewhere in the Universe, precisely what you need is lined up and ready to serve you, just waiting to be asked.

This concept is easy to work with because it utilizes a template you are already comfortable with. Your conscious mind is familiar with the process of hiring from the physical Yellow Pages, so to imagine doing the same thing in the nonphysical dimension is also a simple process. Suddenly, connecting with Spirit becomes as conceivable as any other endeavor. You create the thought, you bring in the talent and energy and ability, and then your request begins to fulfill itself.

Contemplate for a moment how easily some things just fall into place as if they were meant to be, how chance meetings serendipitously occur as if written in a play. What about the way you sometimes get an impulse to go somewhere that puts you in the perfect place at the perfect time? Wouldn't it be wonderful to increase the frequency of these amazing so-called coincidences? That's what can happen every day when you open the Universal Yellow Pages and let the Universe arrange and orchestrate the details of your intentions.

Think Heavens First

On the physical plane we always seem to be dealing with limited resources: not enough money, not enough time, not enough people or experts. If we switch our perception to the Universe, those restrictions don't apply, so just imagine that you have all the money, time, and resources in the world to hire whatever kind of assistance your mind can come up with.

Let's say you're planning a trip to another country. I encourage you to think about the heavenly resource pool *first* and hire a spiritual travel agent and a spiritual activities coordinator to help make it the most enjoyable visit ever. But don't stop there. Remember, your invisible helpers can facilitate anything you think of. You can bring in a spiritual tour guide to show you around, a spiritual translator to bridge the language gap, and a spiritual comedian to make sure there's plenty of laughter during the trip.

Likewise, if you want a new house, think Heavens first and hire a spiritual real-estate agent.

Ready for a better job? Get some inspiration from a spiritual job hunter.

Looking for a new car? Hire a spiritual car salesman.

Feeling overextended? Ask for a spiritual time manager.

Having trouble with your computer? Requisition a spiritual computer tutor to figure out how to solve the problem.

Feeling uneasy about driving in an unfamiliar neighborhood alone? Call spiritual 911 and request a celestial police escort.

Are you getting a feel for this? You can enhance every aspect of your life by tapping into the aptitudes of the Universe. Help from the Divine can facilitate everything you do. Think Heavens first, and you'll thank Heavens!

Angels for Hire

My guidance wants you to know that there are thousands of unemployed angels. Don't ever think your problem is too trivial for you to call upon divine assistance. Don't ever think you might be bothering the celestial helpers. You're not bothering them; you're giving them a job! Think of the world of Spirit as someone you can talk to about anything — or nothing in particular. There's no reason to put on airs or speak in a stiff, formal voice. Spirit knows you. Be real, be spontaneous, be silly — be anything that makes you feel close to this incredibly warm and loving energy. Know that Spirit is honored to be included in every detail of your life. Truly, this is where you'll find unconditional love and the best friend you could ever have.

Angel Express Card

To make the Hiring the Heavens process even more fun and familiar, imagine that you've been given an Angel Express Card, a celestial credit card (with *no* credit limit) that is accepted everywhere. It's at your disposal, and with it you can hire invisible assistants to help advance your dreams and goals, your projects, your relationships, your life's work, your spur-of-the-moment fun.

On page 119, you'll find a couple of Angel Express Cards, whimsical reminders that these resources are always abundantly available, everywhere you go. Put one in your wallet and never leave home without it!

hire Away

Now that you've got your Angel Express Card, you're ready to begin hiring. You'll appreciate the fact that when you hire in the spiritual realm, there are no applications to review, no résumés to read, and no appointments to make. The hiring process is as simple and effortless as your imagination. Think back to when you were a kid. As children, we never had any trouble imagining our most exciting adventures and fantastic wishes. Asking for what we wanted was second nature. Can you remember playing in your own world, one that was filled with imaginary characters? Perhaps you were a castaway on an island, saved by a group of friendly villagers. Perhaps you were a detective, certain you were close to solving the case with the fortuitous assistance of passing street vendors. Whatever your game was, you knew you could create characters at will, even change them midstory if it suited your plot. You never dreamed there were any restrictions on how many characters you could involve or their level of prestige. If you wanted a king or a pauper, you just imagined them.

That's what hiring in the spiritual realm is like. Bring out the child in you and imagine the most fantastic adventure you can. Experience your day-to-day life with a secret world *inside* your world that is assisting you at every turn. Loosen your belt of restrictions and drop any notions of limitation. Open the Universal Yellow Pages and have fun as you expand your mind and discover that you can access whatever energy you wish to bring in, no holds barred. You may find that visualization works for you, and you can picture handing your celestial hires their job descriptions. Or it may feel more natural to you to simply make a verbal request like "I could really use an expert for this situation." It doesn't matter what method you use! The only requirement is your intention. Simply intend, and the assistance will be there. Remember that help is there for any and every aspect of your life — from the mundane to the profound.

Dare to Dream Your Biggest Dream

As adults we stop dreaming and imagining because we think we have to figure out how it will all happen. We are inhibited by the rules and statistics of other people's lives. I encourage you to leave the *how* up to your celestial workforce. Whenever other people tell you what is or isn't possible according to their experience or understanding, silently say, "Yes, but that's not true in my world." Smile to yourself, knowing that your spiritual power team isn't restricted by those rules and statistics. All things are possible from a place of grace. So go ahead and dare to dream the biggest dream you can imagine. Go for it even if they say it can't be done. You are a creator, and the

Heavens will part the seas and roll out the red carpet to support you. Dare to ask for the unrealistic, the impossible, the outrageous. Dare to expand your horizons to the Heavens, where all things are possible.

As Robert Browning said, "Ah, but a man's reach should exceed his grasp, or what's Heaven for?"

...And Your Smallest

Likewise, we often stop ourselves from seeking assistance because we think our requests are too small. We feel awkward asking the Universe to go to all the trouble of arranging circumstances just to our liking. Imagine asking the Powers That Be to arrange the weather for a special day, or to clear the traffic ahead so we can get to an appointment on time. Isn't that a bit selfish? Do we think the whole world revolves around us? The real truth is, yes! The whole world does revolve around every one of us. If we are indeed creating our world in each moment anyway, why not create it the way we want it to be? When we realize this, we understand that far from being selfish or conceited, we are joyfully fulfilling our God-given assignment. Could we possibly think it's somehow more righteous to create something that makes us unhappy? Be assured that the Universe delights in arranging every little detail for the express purpose of putting a smile on your face, a twinkle in your eye, and a skip in your step.

CHAPTER 4

Heavenly Hiring in *action*

J ust imagine the possibilities! It's such a comfort to know that no matter what challenge you are facing, big or small, help is just a thought away. Given all the tremendous stresses of our busy lives, it's easy to feel alone, with nowhere to turn for help. Not anymore! You will soon have a whole new awareness and appreciation for the tremendous support the Universe has to offer you.

Stories from the Spiritual Temp-Agency Files

Let's get an idea of how the fantastic assistance of celestial helpers has worked for other people. These true-life examples of the heavenly hiring practice deal with what I call the Spiritual Temp Agency. This is the placement agency that handles your quick-hires whenever you have a specific short-term need. Since I've been teaching these principles, dozens of people have enthusiastically shared their delightful stories with me.

A SPIRITUAL SLEUTH

I met my friend Deb for lunch one afternoon and told her all about hiring spiritual helpers. When I saw her again a month later, she couldn't wait to tell me what had happened. "I'd been outside gardening for several hours," she said. "When I came into the house, my daughter noticed that the pearl was missing from the ring my husband had given me thirteen years ago. I felt instantly that it was gone forever, lost somewhere in the leaves, grass, or gravel. My heart sank. I thought I had no chance of finding it, so I didn't even try. Then I remembered what you had told me, and I quickly hired a spiritual jewelry sleuth. I asked her to find my pearl and bring it to me. Two hours later, as I was sitting on the bed talking with my kids, our dog, Callie, jumped up to join us. One of the kids said, 'Mom, Callie's playing with something in her mouth,' so I held out my hand and ordered her to drop it. And would you believe she dropped the missing pearl right in front of my hand?"

Deb's story sounds quite miraculous, to say the least. But I've shared her example of the willingness of Spirit to rush to our aid during many of my talks and subsequently have heard story after story from people who hired the spiritual jewelry sleuth to find rings and other pieces of jewelry under the most challenging circumstances. It seems that as soon as the jewelry sleuth's "phone number" was discovered, she was in high demand. If you have any such need, please don't hesitate to call her. I can wholeheartedly promise she's the best in the Universe!

A SPIRITUAL SPEECH COACH

After hearing me speak at a convention, an attendee named Joan called to share how she had put Hiring the Heavens into action. One day, with no warning whatsoever, she was asked to fill in for a sick colleague and give a report on her company's financial plan. Although she knew the plan pretty well, she found speaking in front of a group quite intimidating. And of course she had nothing prepared.

So she dashed into the bathroom, hired a spiritual speech coach on the double, and ended up giving the talk of her life. People even came up afterward to thank her for explaining things so clearly.

A SPIRITUAL PET FINDER

Karen takes care of an elderly neighbor. One morning as she was leaving for work, she found the neighbor crying because her beloved dog, her only companion in life, was lost.

Karen wondered how she could leave under the circumstances, so she quickly went to her car and hired a spiritual pet finder. She visualized the dog wandering around the neighborhood and then watched it guided home, finally imagining it back in her neighbor's arms. Then she went to work, reassuring her neighbor that everything would be taken care of. She had total faith that the dog would be found.

That evening she returned to the neighbor's house, and the phone rang right when she entered. The dog was safe and sound, found by a friend down the street. Karen had been able to put in a full day's work without a bit of worry because she knew the spiritual pet finder was on the job.

A SPIRITUAL PARK RANGER

Steven decided to Hire the Heavens before a trip to Yosemite National Park with his wife. They planned to go there on retreat, and so they particularly wanted their stay to be peaceful and in tune with nature.

Knowing that Yosemite can be very crowded, before leaving, Steven hired a spiritual park ranger and requested that their campsite be a quiet, sacred place. Later he reported that their trip was absolutely magical and exquisitely peaceful. In fact, during their entire four days there, they heard a dog bark twice and didn't cross paths with a single human soul.

A SPIRITUAL HOMEWORK ASSISTANT

Rachel found out that you can even hire for someone else! Her twelve-year-old son, Logan, chose to do a school report on Joe Montana, but he couldn't find any information at the school library. So Rachel drove him to the city library and waited outside with her two-year-old daughter while Logan searched inside. After about an hour he returned almost crying because he couldn't find any books on Joe Montana. Rachel calmly told him to go back inside and look one more time.

As he reluctantly turned to go back inside, she quickly hired a spiritual homework assistant to go with him and help him find the book he needed. Three minutes later Rachel entered the library to see Logan at the checkout counter with an 18 x 11–inch book with a picture of Joe and the title *Montana* on the cover in big, bold letters. "Where did you find this?" she asked incredulously. With eyes wide, Logan spoke as if he couldn't believe what he was about to say. "I went back to the sports section, and I thought to myself, 'What if a book fell behind the racks?' So I poked my head inside the rack and saw a book up on its edge. I reached down and pulled up this book!"

AND MORE...

Katie and her husband were buying a brand-new home. Their hearts were set on a prime lot, but they had to wait for an opportunity to bid on it. Katie was worried that someone else would beat them to it, so she hired a spiritual real estate agent to hold it in their name. She waited on pins and needles for an entire week before their turn came up, and she could hardly sleep the night before. But sure enough, when the time came, the lot was still available. Katie was quite certain this was not a coincidence.

Nancy kept receiving an error message on her computer screen when she attempted to send her financial transmission. In desperation she hired a spiritual computer expert to open the network and send her transmission through. It was successful on the very next attempt.

Judy's car wouldn't start. She was walking back to the house to tell her husband when she thought of hiring a spiritual mechanic. She abruptly did an about-face and returned to her car. Lo and behold, it started right up.

These examples show how even the little things can be facilitated by the Divine. When synchronicities like this happen in your life, you might wonder if it is indeed the spiritual realm working for you, but over time you'll notice that they happen so often that all your skepticism will fade.

Spiritual Committees: The Real Deal

You'll only be getting a glimpse of what Hiring the Heavens can do if you stop with the Spiritual Temp Agency. Many of your intentions and projects can benefit from far more than a single assistant. You can organize an entire workforce or committee to facilitate your long-term endeavors. Remember, you have an enormous resource pool at your disposal. I find working with spiritual committees the most powerful and life-changing aspect of the Hiring the Heavens concept. They can become your constant support team, working right beside you to ensure success in the most incredible ways. Some committees can help you for weeks or months at a time, while others can become lifelong companions. I'm sure you'll enjoy these stories about a few of the ways other people have used spiritual committees for achieving their larger goals in life.

A SPIRITUAL ROMANCE COMMITTEE

Patty was dating an accountant, but she didn't feel he was meant to be her life partner. Widowed years earlier, she had raised two children on her own. Now she wanted a match made in Heaven — and nothing less would do.

Since she had long believed that angels helped her with every aspect of life, Patty called together what she named the Romance Angels and the Creator of Love. She asked that they send to her door someone with the "same heart" as hers and confirm that he was the one by having two significant dates in his life match two significant dates in hers. Then she went about the business of preparing for the love of her life. First she said good-bye to the accountant. Then she did some spring housecleaning. She made room in her closets for her future suitor's belongings and even bought a beautiful frame to hold a picture of the two of them. Next she went wild and bought some luxurious red satin sheets for her bed — along with a matching red teddy. All of this took about a month.

Around this time a neighbor made an appointment for an out-of-state contractor, also widowed, to assess Patty's home. And that's how Mike came to her door. Patty looked into his eyes and saw his kind soul. It was love at first sight. On their first date she found out that Mike's son was born on her birthday, while her son was born on the birthday of Mike's late wife. That took care of the two matching dates! Five days later they confessed their love to each other. They have been inseparable ever since. Truly, theirs is a match made in Heaven.

A SPIRITUAL LIFE-PATH COMMITTEE

Sherry was at the point of utter frustration. For her whole adult life she had wanted to be a professional in the natural healing field, but she had spent most of her time working for others as a receptionist. She had plenty of credentials and personal experience, but for one reason or another, things had just never come together for her. All that changed when she found out about Hiring the Heavens. Thrilled at the thought of getting celestial assistance, she immediately asked for an entire spiritual workforce. Leaving no stone unturned, she hired a promoter, an organizer, a time manager, a financial consultant, and many others to make her dream come true.

Within a matter of weeks things began to happen. She found an office one mile from her home that was being used by a chiropractor. He was open to bringing in other professionals, so with Sherry at the helm they turned the office into a healing arts center and school. Specialists in various areas of natural healing magically appeared, wanting to work in the new office. Sherry was overjoyed with the quality of the practitioners who were being attracted. She watched in amazement as her once-distant, seemingly unreachable dream began to materialize with head-spinning speed.

In Sherry's words, "I went from a lifetime of wishing, wanting, trying, and failing, to practically overnight success!"

But that's not all. Sherry's husband hired a spiritual life-path committee at the same time. For sixteen years he had worked in a ho-hum job just to get a paycheck. Although he had always been fascinated with psychology, he had never pursued it. Within a few weeks of hiring his committee, he discovered a branch of psychology that focuses on happiness rather than on problems. Soon after that, he got a job as a counselor — and he is absolutely passionate about his new profession. He knows without a doubt that this is what he was born to do.

A SPIRITUAL CONFERENCE COMMITTEE

Every year my friend Elizabeth organizes a large conference. She used to find it quite stressful, but as soon as she heard about Hiring the Heavens, she put together a spiritual committee. Among her team of specialists were a spiritual conference director and a spiritual university liaison. She happily reported to me that the latest conference came together with far more ease than in previous years. But she was especially pleased with the spiritual "energy monitor" she had hired to maintain her stamina and make sure she enjoyed herself as an attendee of the conference. It turns out she couldn't stop smiling the whole week.

A SPIRITUAL JOY COMMITTEE

When Gary heard about Hiring the Heavens, he immediately asked for a joy committee to look after him and make his life happier and more bountiful. He had recently been through some rough years with sketchy finances and a divorce. Even though he had retired, he still felt life was extremely demanding, and he just didn't want it to continue that way. Quite emphatically he explained to his joy commit-tee, "Hey, I'm an old guy here. Life shouldn't be this hard. Can't we make things a bit easier on me?"

He now says he can't begin to count the positive ways that moment changed his life. Instead of struggling all the time, he experiences synchronicities on a daily basis and marvels at how things keep working out with ease. When trying to find an address in an unfamiliar area, for example, he has ended up on the right street seemingly by accident. More profound personal changes have taken place in his life as well. For one, in the past he had quite a temper, but since hiring his joy committee, he can't recall a single disgruntled thought or episode of anger. His worries have vanished, replaced by a newfound sense of calmness and comfort that's unshakable. Truly his days are filled with joy.

CHAPTER 5

The Pivotal *moment*

By now you may be wondering how in the world this whole idea came about. Have you ever had an experience that no amount of coincidence could explain, one that was so serendipitous it left you reeling in amazement? You can either dismiss moments like that as unexplainable, attaching no particular meaning to them, or you can take notice of them and let them change your life. Well, what happened to me several years ago, in 1996, did change my life in every way.

At the time, I was working in my own business as a natural health practitioner. I had been taught that our bodies have all the answers to our health concerns and simply need someone to ask the right questions. That's where I came in. Instead of assessing my clients' health from an intellectual viewpoint, my purpose was to help them find their own resolutions. This often led to the discovery of some very interesting hidden core issues, including emotional imbalances and self-sabotaging mental concepts. (And I have certainly participated in my share of miracles by helping people to just connect with the innate wisdom of their own bodies.)

I have learned that there are many ways — such as muscle testing or dowsing with a pendulum — of asking the body yes/no questions and getting it to answer. Working with those answers through a process of elimination, you can narrow the possibilities down to a core issue that's probably causing the discomfort or disease. And that's precisely the point I reached one day with a client named Sam. We had determined that he was experiencing an energetic disharmony with neurotransmitters. (An energetic disharmony is just a fancy way of saying that something wasn't at ease in his body, and a neurotransmitter is a substance that transmits nerve impulses — essentially sensations — in the brain.) I was somewhat vague on the subject of neurotransmitters, but his body insisted that I deal with five of them, and furthermore I needed to identify them. I was stumped. I was able to come up with four (norepinephrin, serotonin, melatonin, and GABA), but I couldn't identify the last one — and I had no idea where to look.

Then out of the blue my client asked, "Is histamine a neurotransmitter?" Since I wasn't that familiar with neurotransmitters, my first reaction was that a layperson like my patient probably would have even less knowledge on the subject. So, I quickly responded in my most professional voice, "No. Histamine is that substance your sinuses produce during an allergic reaction. You know, that's why you take antihistamines." Then, for no reason at all, I had the impulse to turn around and pull a health care book off the shelf, a book I had purchased a year earlier but had never read or even noticed since. I opened to a page somewhere in the middle and laughed when I looked at it because the word *histamine* was in the chapter title. Immediately my eyes fell on a single line buried in a paragraph halfway down that said, "Histamine is also thought to be a neurotransmitter."

I was astounded! How did this happen? Clearly, it was not just some incredible coincidence. Oh no, it was too precise, too specific. Just imagine what had to take place for those events to occur. First, something had to whisper *histamine* to my client. Then, when I dismissed it, some force had to compel me to turn around, pull a never-read book off the shelf, and open to the exact page that would set me straight. Suddenly I became acutely aware that I was not alone. I felt both goose-bumpy and exhilarated. Imagine having the support of unseen wisdom! Was it possible I had a "spiritual physician" assisting me? The very thought gave me an incredible sense of comfort, along with a new awareness that more was going on than met the eye.

Divine Assistance

From that point on I began to notice other evidence that I was getting help from higher sources, and I made a clear decision *not* to dismiss it as mere coincidence. The idea that I had my own spiritual physician to advise me began to take hold. I became aware of a heightened intuition that gave me inside information beyond my technical training. Eventually I came to rely on that inner knowing first, while my education took a backseat. I began to imagine that I had an entire team of physicians looking over my shoulder, advising me at every turn. Needless to say, my work moved to a whole new level.

My clients and I were amazed as unexpected information just appeared in my awareness, seemingly out of the blue. Invariably it would be exactly the missing piece that made all the difference. Sometimes I was guided to suggest remedies that I would not have initially considered, yet they ended up being the perfect solution.

After numerous such experiences, my natural skepticism gave way to an increasing enthusiasm for nurturing divine guidance in my life. Over time I have learned to surrender to that inner voice with all my clients, letting it show me what needs to be done. Some might suggest that my own intellect, or maybe my subconscious mind, is generating the information, but I *know* it comes from a divine source. Often I feel like merely an observer, witnessing the incredible interplay between my client and my spiritual physician working through me. I am intuitively guided to the knowledge that illuminates the mysteries of each client's condition and allows me to offer them precisely the right remedies.

Support Staff

Paying attention to this guidance worked so well in treating my clients that I began to wonder if my guides would like to help out with other aspects of my business. For example, I needed a secretary, a marketing representative, and a book-keeper. Wondering if those positions could possibly be filled on a spiritual rather than a physical level, I put out a requisition to see what would happen. I imagined asking the Universe for angelic assistants who had just the right talents and abilities to joyously perform the required functions.

Then I started holding imaginary staff meetings in my car on the way to work. Out loud, I would talk to my group of spiritual physicians, health professionals, and newly hired office staff about our intentions for the day — who our clients were, what we would be working on, and so forth. I would fill them in on the details of my business just as if I were speaking with an earthly staff.

Sure enough, after hiring my spiritual secretary, marketing rep, and bookkeeper, my practice flourished with incredible ease. My paperwork and billing didn't magically calculate, print, and mail itself, but somehow I found myself taking care of it with complete ease, and in record time. With my spiritual team by my side, I have all the business I want, my schedule flows smoothly, and my clients are delighted with their results.

Here are some fun stories about how my life has changed since I added my heavenly office staff.

FIELD MY CALLS!

Every summer I attend a weeklong convention in Santa Cruz, California. I used to spend every morning, every lunch break, and every evening on my cell phone listening to messages and returning client phone calls. If I didn't retrieve and delete those messages, my answering machine would actually reach a cutoff point. But then I realized that my stellar staff could lend a helping hand. "This is the perfect job for my celestial secretary," I thought.

So when the next convention rolled around, I asked her to hold my calls to no more than five or six during the entire event. And lo and behold, I found exactly six messages waiting for me when I got home.

BOOK ME UP!

Since hiring my spiritual marketing rep, I have all the clients I want, in spite of the fact that I don't advertise. But one Friday morning I flipped the page of my appointment calendar and discovered that the following week was only about half full. So I called an emergency staff meeting and earnestly pleaded with my marketing rep to get on the horn and book me up. By that afternoon I had twenty-three calls requesting appointments.

FINANCIAL SUPPORT

If you're like me, you can definitely use some divine intervention in this area! All I can tell you is that I'm amazed at how abundantly money flows for me now, and how it just isn't the worry it used to be. Whatever I need to do for my business, be it a seminar I'd like to attend or a new piece of equipment I need to buy, the money is always there.

Personal Staff

By 1997, one year after my first experiences with celestial helpers, my work had become a breeze! I had grown comfortable with the notion that not only did Spirit *want* me to do this work, it offered me generous support as well.

At that point I decided to pull out all the stops. Was it possible to receive help in *all* areas of my life? Naturally, as soon as I asked, evidence of divine assistance began showing up in spades.

Not only did my business life flow more smoothly than ever, but my personal life did as well. I now have helpers for shopping, home projects, family issues, personal emotional challenges, social events, recreation, vacations, and more.

A SPIRITUAL WARDROBE CONSULTANT

Ladies, don't miss this story. Believe it or not, clothes shopping used to be one of my least favorite activities — so much so that I had to be desperate before venturing into the wilds of malls and department stores. I never seemed to find any clothes I liked. They didn't fit right, they cost too much, and I ended up exhausted and frustrated.

Finally I realized that with the help of a creative Spirit, I could change that experience to one of pleasure and success. The next time I went looking for clothes, I hired a spiritual wardrobe consultant to accompany me. Let me tell you, dahling, he was mahvelous. I felt guided to pick nothing but gems from the numerous racks, just as though I had an earthly personal shopper by my side. Instead of an exercise in frustration, clothes shopping became one of excitement and delight. I found outfit after outfit that I couldn't wait to try on. So many turned out to be just my style and size that I was faced with a new dilemma — what *not* to buy. I'm almost embarrassed to admit that I bought seventeen outfits that day for just over two hundred dollars. Now that's a personal shopper with a bargain in mind.

Since that time I always hire spiritual shopping assistants to help me out. They guide me to the perfect store and the perfect item. This comes in especially handy during the

Christmas rush, when I need to find the best gifts in the short-est amount of time. And like the icing on the cake, they even help me find parking spaces during those busy times of year!

A SPIRITUAL VACATION TEAM

My children wanted to take a vacation, but as those of you who are parents know, family trips can be so exhausting that you need a vacation after your vacation. All of that changed when I hired an entire team to help along the way. I had a spir-itual mechanic to keep the van running safely, a spiritual travel agent to help me find excellent accommodations, and a spiri-tual gourmet to pick out fantastic restaurants while keeping an eye on our budget. But my favorite hire, and the one I've kept as part of my permanent staff, was the attitude adjuster. Can you imagine taking a ten-hour drive with four kids without any bickering? It was heaven! My husband and I enjoyed the best vacation ever, and the kids can't wait to do it again.

A SPIRITUAL BOOK-WRITING COMMITTEE

On a more serious note, I can't imagine how I could have written this book without the incredible assistance of the celestial realm. First of all, even though I had thought many times of writing on other subjects, the task always proved too overwhelming. I had very little confidence that I could actually finish a book. I had always considered myself more of an idea person; I had pages of concepts and titles, but had never even come close to bringing any of them to fruition.

So when I was inspired to write a book about the Hiring the Heavens process, I immediately recruited a specialized spiritual committee to pave the way. I knew I would have to hone new skills, change the way I viewed myself, and grow in all kinds of ways. And that's exactly what has happened. On top of that, the help I've received from top-notch earthly professionals has been extraordinary every step of the way. The most amazing part is that most of them were *brought to me* without my having to physically seek them out. (Only when I got impatient and tried to force matters did I get sidetracked: see "Be Patient" in chapter 7.) Truly, this book was written using the exact process it describes.

Let me elaborate. I had written an outline and some of the material (enough to begin giving talks on the subject), but I still felt inept at fleshing out the contents. I asked my spiritual project committee to find me someone who could help shape my ideas and bring new life to the words. I asked that this person be fully appreciative of the concept and aware of how it could work. Two days later I received a phone call from a complete stranger who had heard about me from a mutual friend. She introduced herself as a developmental editor and asked if I was working on any projects. Of course I hired her right away, confident that the Universe had arranged our meeting. She turned out to have exactly the abilities I had asked for. In addition to that, she introduced me to the writings and audiotapes of Abraham-Hicks. Esther Hicks is an inspirational speaker who communicates with a group of spiritual teachers who call themselves Abraham. If you have not heard of them, I encourage you to seek them out on the internet, at www.abraham-hicks.com. You'll be amazed, as I was, at how closely some of their teachings harmonize with the concepts in this book. I was absolutely blown away to have such a gifted developmental editor virtually placed in my lap, one who was completely comfortable with the ideas in my book.

Once that initial phase was completed, I needed to find someone who could help me expand, organize, and polish the book. Again I asked my spiritual committee to bring the perfect person to me. The very next day a new client came into my office and introduced herself as a copy editor. We hit it off instantly, and I hired her on the spot, knowing that our meeting was no accident. And once again, she had exactly the abilities I needed! But I was floored a month later when she revealed that she too was a fan of Abraham-Hicks. It turns out she had been inspired by their teachings for years. What are the chances of having two exceptional editors with similar philosophical backgrounds propelled my way? Both of them were truly heaven-sent.

The next part of the story is even better. Eventually, my spiritual committee started giving me the nudge that it was time to submit my book to a publisher. I had already done enough research to know how competitive the field was and that the chances of a first-time author being picked up by a major publishing house were slim to none. The industry leaders will tell you that the best way to increase your chances is to take a class on how to write a book proposal and marketing plan that will hopefully entice the publisher to give your book a second look. And they say to submit your work to at least thirty different publishers and to not be discouraged if you are turned down by all of them.

By now you know, though, that when you hire the Heavens you can get inside information that puts you way ahead of the pack. I simply asked my spiritual book-writing committee to guide me to the perfect publisher. Then, I went to my bookshelves and prompted, "Show me a book that was published by this perfect choice." My eyes immediately fell on *The Power of Now* published by New World Library in Novato, California. Excitedly, I looked up New World Library on the internet and became convinced that it was the ideal home for *Hiring the Heavens.*

I did no further research on any other publishers, and I didn't submit to any others. All I did was send my book — without even a formal book proposal or marketing plan — to New World Library with full confidence that my spiritual committee would pave the way. And of course, New World Library called. My book was placed with the perfect publisher, exemplifying the very process of which it speaks. You see, with the power of the Heavens behind you, there's no telling what you can do that will defy the statistics. I was absolutely thrilled, and I congratulated my spiritual book-writing committee for a job well done.

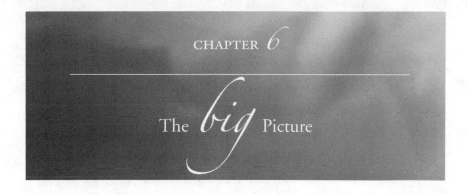

CHAPTER 6

The *big* Picture

Intrigued by the evidence of spiritual help that started show-ing up in every aspect of my life, I began to wonder how my Hiring the Heavens process differed from prayer. After all, people had been asking God for help throughout the ages. So I picked up pencil and paper and asked to be shown a picture of what was going on. Here's what I got.

The Old Paradigm:
God Above, Self Below

In the old paradigm, the one with which many of us grew up, God is up above — with all the power — while the Self is down below. Any communication is usually upward, with the Self asking God for something. For example, typical prayers might be, "God, please heal my son," "God, please help me with my finals," or "God, please bless Aunt Sue."

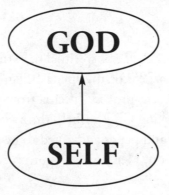

This, however, was clearly not the paradigm from which I operated when hiring a spiritual workforce. Once I realized this, I tried to figure out what the dynamics in my process were so I could identify a new paradigm. So what was it then?

The New Paradigm: Attempt #1

I decided to try putting the divine helpers (shown as stars in the following illustration) in a circle between God up there and Self down here — as middle management, so to speak. In this model, the Self worked through spiritual intercessors to talk to God, who still had all the power.

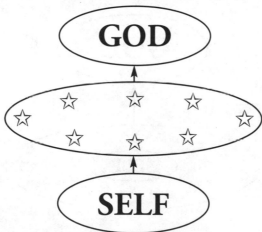

I asked my inner guidance if this was correct, and what I got back was *You're not even close.*

The New Paradigm: Attempt #2

So I tried again. In this version God remained up above, while the Self moved into the circle of guides, angels, and celestial assistants — the Spirits of Creation — to become part of middle management. Here the Self began to have decision-making power.

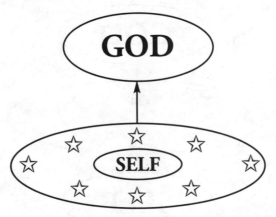

I asked if this was correct. Once again I was told it was not.

The New Paradigm: Attempt #3

I tried a third time. I put the Self in the upper part of the circle, connected by lines to the spiritual workforce below it. Here the Self clearly had a support staff, while God remained above it all.

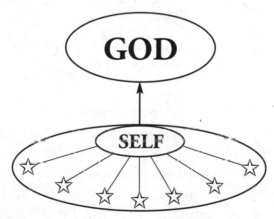

Again I asked my guidance, and again I was told, *No, that's not it either.*

The New Paradigm: Attempt #4

I scratched my head, wondering what I was missing. What else could I possibly do? Then, in a moment of inspiration, I was guided to pick up my pencil and place God right there in the circle with the rest of the staff.

Full of doubt, I asked my guidance, "Is this what you're trying to show me?" The answer, finally, was, *Yes, that's it.*

I sat back in disbelief, feeling rather intense trepidation. Who was I to think that the entire spiritual realm, including God, was there to support *me,* that I could be that significant? Based upon my strict fundamentalist upbringing, this was blasphemy! I thought long and hard about the picture that sat before me. "What's really being said here?" I asked.

Frantically my mind began searching for a familiar analogy here on Earth that might explain this jolting image.

GOD AS A NURTURING PARENT

In reply to my impassioned query, I was led to these observations.

As children we exist very much in the first paradigm. Our parents are God figures in our lives. We look to them to meet all our needs and provide all our answers. They give us very specific directions that we must obey and follow.

But that doesn't work when we're nineteen, does it? At some point we say, "Mom, Dad, I've got to fly with my own wings. This is my life, and I've got to live it my way. But I do appreciate knowing that you're always there for me and that I can always come home."

And can you imagine the old paradigm working when we're thirty-five? At that point we're clearly in charge of our lives, and the degree to which our parents are involved is fully up to us. Most parents would be extremely frustrated if their thirty-five-year-old children continued to live at home, insisting upon parental guidance instead of venturing out on their own. This progression from dependent child to independent adult represents the natural order of things. No one questions it.

CONNECTING THE DOTS

When I extended the image of leaving the nest from the physical family to the spiritual family, the dots began to connect. This analogy was the starting point from which I eventually reconciled for myself the message of the new paradigm. Let me share some of my thought process with you.

As a child I was told that God had a plan for me. I was taught that since my free will was imperfect, I should let Him determine the course of my life. I accepted this old-paradigm worldview, which regards humans as lacking in resources and discernment.

Over time, and especially in the process of writing this book, I've come to see things differently. I see the new paradigm eclipsing the old. And from this expanded perspective we require a restructured relationship with God.

The new paradigm depicts a God who wants His children to freely and courageously fulfill their assignments on this planet. As a parent, He wants us to grow up prepared to make our own decisions and live our own lives. He wants us to shine the light of our power and our divinity, knowing we have access to divine guidance and assistance every step of the way.

Unfortunately, many people expect to be struck down by lightning for merely contemplating that they could be one with Spirit. To insinuate that they have the creative power of God is tantamount to heresy. On the other hand, I (like so many others) have come to believe that all of us are wondrous and perfect creations, inherently qualified to stand at the helm of our lives, certain of our jurisdiction. In fact...I've come to the conclusion that blasphemy lies only in our *rejection* of this power.

DIVINE DESIGN

With that in mind, I invite you to shift your focus to your true nature within and look with fresh eyes upon the reality of your divine power. Could it be that God's only plan for us is that we accept our promotion and take full responsibility in the office of our lives? When we call upon God or the spiritual realm, divine guidance will always be there to inspire and support us (just as a loving parent would be). But we are being asked to grow up spiritually and find the courage to take charge of our own lives.

The Final Drawing

I'll say it again: By divine design we are creators with God, literally in the director's chair of our life. God and the entire spiritual realm are part of our support system, the wellspring of all our resources.

The following drawing, a refinement of Attempt #4, came forth unexpectedly one March morning. I was staying in a beautiful Lake Tahoe condominium with a couple of girlfriends, one of whom was my developmental editor. I had invited her along so that we could spend several days work-ing on the book. We were sitting at the computer, where she was trying to re-create the pencil drawings I had made of my attempts at figuring out the new paradigm. I watched the computer screen as she placed the word *God* in the illustra-tion. She was trying to paste it in among the stars when...

poof! *God* just popped in where He wanted to be: the *o* in *God* was replaced with the circle around *Self.* No kidding, the letters *G* and *D* actually grew in size and jumped into the background, becoming partially obscured by the larger circle and reminding us of the sunrise that gives birth to each new day.

We're still not sure how it happened, but we instantly recognized its perfection. We saw that God is the context in which all of our lives occur, the Source that gives rise to everything we experience. And we saw that God in turn experiences *through us* — an epiphany of the highest order. The new paradigm was there, right before our eyes.

The striking distinction between this model and its predecessor is the implication that we are an integral part, an extension even, of God, and that as such, we are being asked to consciously create our own world, fully confident in our seat of authority — *and* in our knowledge that the entire Universe stands joyfully ready to assist us.

CHAPTER 7

Hiring as the *creator*

Are you ready to take command as creator? Then it's time to roll up your sleeves and begin consciously and deliberately creating your experience as God intends. This is the fun part! To get your feet wet, start with something very simple that will only require the assistance of the Spiritual Temp Agency, something that can be fulfilled within the very first day (or even within minutes). Take a moment to think of a matter you'd like some help with. Perhaps you need to buy a birthday present and want a gift angel to inspire you with the perfect idea. Maybe you're feeling a little down and could use a pep rally from the celestial cheerleaders. Or perhaps you've lost your wallet and want a spiritual sleuth to find it for you. Remember that your intention is the key. In the following paragraphs you'll find some helpful suggestions to facilitate success at every turn. The first step is just to...

Ask!

The fantastic assistance of the Universe will elude you unless you ask for it. We all know how easy it is to feel frustrated when we're having trouble managing some aspect of our life. We may throw up our hands, lamenting, "Why is this happening to me?" or "I wish I had this or that." But that's not asking; that's complaining. Ask with intention and *trust the Universe to support you.* The door can then open wide for a serendipitous solution to appear.

Don't underestimate the power of the spoken word. Your request will hold more conviction if you say it out loud. Our minds are full of endless chatter. Anyone tuning in would find it difficult to know when we really mean something and when it's just a lot of jumbled rambling. Using our voice helps us get our own attention and focus on what it is we really want. I find that when I speak out loud, my sentences are far more coherent. I imagine a presence, an intelligent energy listening as I explain my request. (I don't picture this energy as a person, or give it a personal name, but you might like to try that. Do whatever works best for you!)

Don't waste even a minute feeling embarrassed. The Universe finds nothing but delight in being involved with every endeavor in your life, and it enthusiastically waits to hear your thoughts and ideas.

Here's something else to keep in mind. Like me, you may have read books and attended seminars that presented very definite rules about how to phrase requests. But those rules don't apply here. When you employ the Heavens, you can relax. Just ask! No matter how you put it, you're not going to get it wrong. There's no test to see who can come up with the fanciest or most precise words. The last thing you want to do is create anxiety about how you're expressing yourself.

For example, some self-help practitioners and lecturers warn us to avoid saying things like "Those chocolates are to die for" or "I'd sell my soul for a house like that" because the Universe might take us literally. This suggests that the Universe, in all its wisdom, can't decipher the true meaning behind our figures of speech! If that were true, we would be creating disaster at every turn. My advice is, don't buy into this belief system. Instead, picture the cosmic forces as loving friends who are easy to talk to, know exactly how you feel, and are hip to what you really mean, no matter what modern lingo you use. (And don't worry: they can understand all foreign languages too!)

For years popular wisdom has advised us on the perfect way to say affirmations. The experts warn against wanting. They urge us to never say "I want a new house on a hill" because the Universe will supposedly match the vibration of our words and leave us wanting eternally, never having that house because we didn't speak it as an affirmative statement in present time. So I learned to say "I now enjoy my beautiful new house on a hill." That, I was assured, was the preferred mantra for success.

But eventually I came to understand that, far from being

an obstacle, wanting is actually an *essential* element in the process of joyfully fulfilling our dreams. Wanting is the seed of desire, and without desire there can be no change, no growth, no creation. I realized that the Universe actually celebrates whenever we identify something we want. Desire is the spark that ignites the force of creation. I'm here to give you permission to want all you want! Seed your dreams, embrace your wishes, and open yourself to the magic of your desires. But don't forget to ask!

. . . And You Shall Receive

This is the other half of the equation. Being open to receiving is just as important as asking. It seems silly to have to point this out, but so many of us stop the flow at this place. We've all heard the saying "It's better to give than to receive," so we think that by refusing to receive, we are somehow being more righteous. The truth is that giving and receiving form a complete cycle. If we stop the flow of one, we stop the flow of the other. When the Universe showers us with blessings, we must be in a state of gracious acceptance. If we decline, thinking that's the virtuous thing to do, we halt the process and stifle our ability to give.

I know a massage therapist who has a fantastic ability to heal pain. But because she believed that her gift came from God, she thought it was inappropriate to charge for her services. Money, she felt, was a lowly human necessity that would taint her divine calling. So even though she asked the Universe to provide her with opportunities to help people, her practice didn't flourish because she couldn't afford to open an office or pay for higher training. Her gift remained hidden from everyone except a few family members. Finally, a friend pointed out that unless she allowed herself to receive monetary compensation, she would never be able to share her talent. In a flash of awareness she realized she'd been interrupting the cycle of giving and receiving and that neither could exist without the other. I'm happy to report that she now has a robust practice and helps many people every day.

Here's another example. My brother Tom wanted to catch an early flight home to Florida. When he discovered that thirty-two people were on the waiting list ahead of him, he hired a spiritual travel agent to open a seat for him. But the next time he inquired, an hour before departure, all thirty-two were still on the list. Half an hour later nothing had changed, so he left the airport and checked in to a hotel. Then, just before going to sleep, he called his girlfriend. She happened to work for the same airline he'd planned to travel on, and out of curiosity she decided to check on the status of the flight. Well, guess what? She was astonished to find that the flight had taken off with one empty seat! My brother's spiritual travel agent had responded to his request, but he wasn't there to receive.

More about Asking

The following are some guidelines you may want to keep in mind when asking, but they are *not* rules. The essential part is to simply *ask*. Use these suggestions as a framework, within which you can seed and nourish your dreams.

BE PLAYFUL

Keep a lighthearted and playful attitude. This life is a joyous creation, meant to be celebrated and filled with the full spectrum of human experience. It shouldn't come as a surprise to know that God really does want us to enjoy our lives, but the fact is many people believe that life is meant to be hard. They feel it is a series of tests, a type of proving ground where they are trying to earn God's favor. With this philosophy they are never good enough, never lovable enough, and always separate from God.

The Hiring the Heavens process, on the contrary, shows that we are the very extensions of God Himself, and as such always good enough, always lovable enough, and never separate. God wants to experience joy and fulfillment through us, and He gives us unlimited support from the Heavens to carry out the yearnings of our soul.

Even so, staying in a constant state of exuberant creation and joy does not mean enjoying perpetual fun to the exclusion of other emotions. We've all had the experience of achieving something very difficult that at the time was anything but fun, yet in the end it was worth every bit of sweat. The joyous expression of our lives means we are free to experiment with the entire banquet of human emotions — and in them find happiness and joy. It may seem strange, but in this frame of mind we can even experience joy in frustration, joy in sadness, and joy in despair.

The joy comes when we recognize that whatever situation we may find ourselves in, it's only a role we are playing. This gives us a playful state of mind that's almost like witnessing ourselves in the third person. It's an observation point that makes us the performer, the producer, and even the audience. Imagine being asked to play a role in a movie where your character falls into the depths of despair. As an actor, you are challenged to dig deep within your creative soul to bring the expression of despair to the screen, but at the same time you feel good about your ability to convey that particular emotion. Life is like that. Life is a play in which we have chosen a role. While we are the actor, we are also the director who playfully decides what will happen next. Even in the midst of our pain we can find joy in our performance, realizing that, as so many wise teachers have said, we truly are spiritual beings having human experiences.

Take a step back and assess the role you are playing in your life. Don't identify with your pain and suffering. Recognize that even when tears are streaming down your face, your true self cherishes you and is honored to be experiencing life through your eyes. From this perspective it's easier to move into a more pleasurable state. And one of the best ways to do that is to...

CULTIVATE AN ATTITUDE OF GRATITUDE

An attitude of thankfulness and appreciation is the essence of joy. Whenever you're feeling down, the quickest way out is to follow that old cliché and count your blessings. As soon as you do, your whole being begins to vibrate at a different rate. Instead of letting your negative attitude attract more of the same unhappiness and despondency, you can shift into hopeful expectation of more blessings to come.

Look for evidence in all your endeavors that the Heavens are orchestrating your desires and intentions. Pay attention to seeming coincidences and synchronicities, even if they appear small, and give credit to your spiritual team. There is no order of difficulty when it comes to miracles. It's just as miraculous for the Universe to arrange the chance meeting of two old friends as it is to heal someone who's sick. Notice all things, big and small, that are miracles in your life. Soon you'll be convinced that Spirit is walking right beside you, paving the way as you go. Express how grateful you are for the extraordinary ways the Spirits of Creation provide their expert advice and skills. Acknowledgment and an attitude of gratitude will evoke continued excitement and expanded support from your already willing celestial task force.

INTEND FOR THE HIGHEST GOOD

Keep your intentions pure. Request that whatever comes be for the highest and greatest good — not just for yourself, but for all concerned. You may say out loud, "I ask that this heavenly assistance be brought to me in just the perfect way, for the highest and greatest good of all concerned," or something similar that feels right to you. I cannot emphasize too strongly how important this will be for your peace of mind. Many people worry that what they desire might ultimately take away from or hurt someone else, but that's not possible if you intend the best for everyone involved. This is a win-win situation where there is always plenty to go around and no shortage of good things or creative solutions. Realize that you can never help others by being or having less.

FEEL YOUR WANTS

Often what we think we want isn't truly what our heart intends. Take a moment to ponder what it is you actually desire, and then put it in terms of feelings. After all, what we really want is the feelings people and things give us, not the possessions themselves. Perhaps you desire someone to share a romantic relationship with. Instead of spelling out what you want this person to look and act like from a material viewpoint, focus on the feelings you wish to generate and the essential qualities that are most important to you. What you truly desire may be mutual attraction and a warm, loving connection with someone who embodies compassion and spontaneity. Rephrase your request, emphasizing those feelings and qualities. Then let the Universe surprise you with a relationship exceeding your wildest dreams. A friend gave me an example of what can happen when you stay in your head and not in your heart. She asked for a dark, handsome, very masculine Marlboro Man. Well, she got her Marlboro Man all right, but then she got tired of his smoking!

Let me give you another example. Perhaps you've been asking to bring in X number of dollars each month because you think it will cover your bills and keep you financially secure. Unfortunately, life doesn't work that way. It always seems that the more money we make, the more we spend, leaving us in exactly the same predicament, except with bigger worries and more daunting bills. Instead, concentrate on the *feeling* you want. Ask for pleasure and ease while paying your bills. Ask for a feeling of security and financial freedom. After all, this is what you truly want. Then let the Universe arrange how it will happen.

HAVE FAITH

You just have to know this is the way the Universe works. *Know* that it will happen. It will not serve any purpose to use this process as a testing ground for the Universe. An "I'll believe it when I see it" attitude will keep success just outside your reach. Spiritual teacher and author Wayne Dyer says, "You'll see it when you believe it." Launch your request to the ether and then simply stay in a state of happy expectancy and appreciation rather than a "prove it" mind-set.

You may say, "Do you really expect me to believe that I can have whatever I ask for?" Well, yes, I do expect you to believe that. This is the essence of true magic. This is the stuff that makes miracles happen and seems to defy the laws of physics. Who says it isn't possible? A perfect example is fire-walking, a practice in which ordinary people are taught how to create a new reality and walk across a bed of fiery red coals without getting burned. How could that be possible if not for their absolute certainty that it was possible? Another example is the placebo effect, which is so well documented that it is even factored into medical studies. Doctors know that the very belief in a treatment is often enough to bring about a cure.

Faith is what makes all things possible. Faith is what sustains the human spirit. Believe it, and you will see it.

STAY UNATTACHED

There's a real art to asking the Universe to fulfill your dreams while staying unattached. I've already talked about how important it is to define your wants and desires, and now I'm going to tell you to let go of them! What does that mean? It means recognizing that your happiness does not depend on whether or not you get what you've asked for. If you become attached, it takes you out of your playful, joyful attitude and into one of need and desperation — even if only on a subtle or subconscious level. This not only keeps you from the joy you could be experiencing during the creative process, it also brings up anxiety about whether or not the Universe is really going to come through for you. "Do I deserve this? Is the Universe listening to me? Will I be happy? Am I good enough?" Fear always constricts your ability to open to the magnificent solutions the Universe has to offer. The more you work with the Hiring the Heavens process, the more you'll replace any anxiety or insecurity with the confidence that you'll always be able to find your joy.

Attachment also creates an expectancy box. As we stir our imagination and generate excitement about what we want, we naturally choose the outcome we think is best. The trouble starts when we get fixated on a certain outcome, going into more and more detail until we've created a box with a predetermined size and shape. We may think the result we've imagined is exactly what we want, but our celestial team has the advantage of a higher perspective. The Universe knows the essence of our desires and can arrange all the particulars. So if what you ask for doesn't manifest quite the way you envisioned it, relax!

Don't try to force it, and don't consider yourself a failure. Instead, know that there's always a reason — and a new opportunity for clarity and creation. Staying unattached allows for the infinitely creative Source to delight you in ways that are even better than you may have imagined.

BE PATIENT

The Universe is usually so immediate in its response to me that when things don't happen as soon as I expect them to, I can get a little impatient. But whenever I try to hurry things along, it ends up costing me *extra* time, money, and effort! Only later, with twenty-twenty hindsight, can I see why the timing had to be orchestrated a certain way so that all the pieces could fall into place. And then I am in awe of its perfection.

Patience is difficult in a society where our technological wizardry so often provides us with instant results. But truly, sometimes various circumstances have to unfold before everything is in alignment. Only from a higher perspective could we possibly understand all that is arranged on behalf of our endeavors. Have patience and know that divine timing is impeccable.

CHAPTER 8

Designing Your *committees*

Okay! We've delved into wanting, desiring, asking, and receiving. And perhaps you've already experimented with hiring from the Spiritual Temp Agency. Now it's time to start exploring your more complicated and longer-term hiring needs, those that can benefit from an entire committee of helpers. In this chapter you'll find a step-by-step process for requisitioning and managing your committee members.

As we saw in chapter 4, working with committees can be

extremely powerful. For example, if you want to improve your health, you might decide to seek guidance from a whole team of spiritual doctors, nutritionists, fitness experts, and weight consultants, who will work behind the scenes to help you serendipitously find the best and most appropriate advisors and caregivers.

Or maybe you'd like to strike out on your own and start a business. In this case you could definitely benefit from the help of a spiritual project manager to arrange "chance" meetings with a mentor, an attorney, a business advisor, and someone to make sure you have all the right connections. You may even need inspiration from a spiritual muse to come up with the perfect name for your business.

Or let's say you're embarking on the grand adventure of building your own home. You might need an earthly architect, contractor, electrician, plumber, and interior decorator, just to name a few. It can be overwhelming when you realize how many different individuals and teams you require on a physical level. But if you hire them first on a spiritual level, you'll launch the energy ahead of time to accomplish your project. And with that, you'll magically bring forth top-notch earthly professionals with exactly the skills and information you need.

You may want to experiment with managerial style. For example, you could personally hire all of your spiritual staff members and meet with them daily, or you could simply hire a spiritual project manager and let her do the rest. In either case, you'll want to maintain close communication and a good working relationship.

The Steps

Here are a few easy steps to follow for hiring committees. Many people find them helpful, but please know that they are in no way necessary for your success. They are an excellent way to organize your thoughts and focus your intentions, but if you would rather just do it all in your head, or in some other way altogether, feel free to use them for inspiration only.

In the back of the book, you'll find some worksheet pages that will make it easy to play with this process. Use them any way that works best for you. For instance, you might want to fill them out right here in the book, or makes copies and create a binder.

SEVEN STEPS FOR HIRING YOUR SPIRITUAL COMMITTEES

1. Name Your Committee
2. Define Your Mission Statement
3. List the Specialists You Wish to Hire
4. Make a Task List
5. Launch Your Committee
6. Hold Staff Meetings
7. Celebrate Your Successes

Now let's look at the nuts and bolts of each step. Remember to have fun with this!

STEP I. NAME YOUR COMMITTEE

Take out a piece of paper and write the title of your spiritual committee on top. For example, let's say you're planning a large dinner party. Catchy committee titles might be the

Epicurean Extravaganza Committee or the Evening with Friends Committee, or you could simply call it the Dinner Committee.

STEP 2. DEFINE YOUR MISSION STATEMENT

Below the title, write a mission statement that describes why you're pulling this committee together. Take some time to get clear about what you want to accomplish. List your goals, your parameters, your requirements, and your budget (if applicable). Make it fun, so you'll look forward to the results.

To continue with the dinner party example, your mission statement might read something like this: *My Dinner Committee will assist me in putting together a fabulous meal for all those who attend and ensuring that everyone, including me, has a great time.*

STEP 3. LIST THE SPECIALISTS YOU WISH TO HIRE

Now put on your thinking cap and start listing all the particular experts and attributes you'd like to include in your committee. This is the point when you pull out your Angel

Express Card and have some fun. Remember that your heavenly help will be standing over your shoulder providing inspiration and arranging the circumstances in magical ways. You can even hire a prompter just to help you think of all the members you'll need to hire for this committee! The list can be as comprehensive as you wish since there's no limit whatsoever to the talent awaiting your request.

The Dinner Committee could use the following members:

- a Chef Extraordinaire to supervise every dish for taste and presentation,

- a Time Manager to orchestrate the meal so that the food reaches the table hot and cooked to perfection,

- a Group Attitude Monitor to make sure everyone is in a pleasant mood and has such a good time that they can't wait to do it again,

- an Etiquette Advisor to envelop the host and hostess with charm and poise,

- a Decorator to add a festive touch of color and warmth to the house,

- a House Cleaner to assist in having the house neat as a pin well before the party,

- and a Food and Beverage Shopper to help prepare the ingredient list and ensure the freshness of the fruits and vegetables.

Have we forgotten anything? Let's hire a Manager for Forgotten Odds and Ends to take care of the little things that can fall through the cracks.

STEP 4. MAKE A TASK LIST

Next, write the task list for your newly hired committee. This is a detailed list that you can amend at any time — and you can check off items as you complete them. It's also a great way to keep track of your progress. Your task list can be a typical to-do list (send out invitations, clean house, prepare shopping list, etc.) that will serve as your own reminder of what needs to be done as well as a prompt for your spiritual helpers to participate in extraordinary ways. You'll feel calm and relaxed knowing that you are getting an extra boost from a higher dimension.

STEP 5. LAUNCH YOUR COMMITTEE

You may want to launch your committee with some sort of ceremony. This isn't a requirement, but it can often make the whole process more fun, focused, and official. Lighting a candle, for example, is a simple form of ceremony. If you have a longer-term project, you can even light one every day to bring in the energy anew. You might decide to initiate the process with some kind of meditation or prayer. Or you can simply call your group together and say, "Here's your mission. Go get 'em." Be creative and have fun!

STEP 6. HOLD STAFF MEETINGS

In the next chapter, I describe in detail how to hold staff meetings. I suggest you do this frequently. Depending on the project, you may want to meet throughout the day or just as the need arises. In my work as a natural health practitioner,

I find daily meetings with my celestial staff essential for setting my intentions and maintaining a close relationship with Spirit.

STEP 7. CELEBRATE YOUR SUCCESSES

Your celestial workforce loves celebration just as much as you do. Be sure to exuberantly acknowledge the many ways your committees have assisted you, giving thanks for their guidance and inspiration.

CHAPTER 9

Conversing with *spirit*

You've pulled together your committee and gone over your task list. Now it's important to know how to talk to the nonphysical dimension and how they will talk to you.

How to Talk to Spirit

One of the best ways to keep in touch with your heavenly hires is through staff meetings. They are invaluable when it comes to managing your creations and forming a close bond with Spirit. Imagine that you're meeting with your group just as you would with an earthly staff. The difference is that you can call these meetings instantaneously, no matter where you are, with no coffee or donuts required!

I hold my staff meetings in the car on my way to work. I talk to my celestial group as if they were sitting right in front of me. I thank them for their exceptional work the day before, saying something like, "Wow, that was awesome how it all came together yesterday. Thank you for the inspiration!" I even sing to them, making up melodies to go with my words of gratitude. This is especially fun for me, and I can tell they find it quite humorous and delightful.

Staff meetings are opportunities to make your requests for the day, ask for inspiration, and ask for the perfect person or piece of information to come along. Imagine a professional staff right in front of you, one that desires guidance and direction from you as well.

When you talk to your celestial staff, express yourself in as natural and real a manner as possible. This down-to-earth approach makes your relationship with Spirit personal and friendly. And know that your life is a work in progress. That means it's okay to refine your request midstream, or to change your mind altogether. As I explained in chapter 7, sometimes the Universe has reasons for manifesting an outcome that isn't quite what you'd had in mind, so it's important not to get too attached to your expectations. However, here I want to point out that you shouldn't hesitate to turn something down after your spiritual workforce has manifested it — even if it is exactly what you asked for. You may realize that it isn't what you need or want after all, so you can revise your request in order to end up with what truly works. For example, I wanted to buy a car, so I asked for a certain model, color, condition, and price, and the very next day I saw a car parked with a FOR SALE sign on it that fit the description. I was blown away because it was exactly what I asked for in every detail. But after looking it over I decided I didn't really like it as much as I thought I would. My spiritual Car Committee showed me how easy it is to bring forth what we ask for — our challenge is to figure out what we truly want! So don't worry about insulting your helpers; their only desire is to bring you joy. You can even admit your weaknesses and express your frustration or anger. Spirit can handle it. You won't be mocked, scoffed at, or struck by lightning. What you *will* receive is amazing support.

The Bible says, "Thy rod and Thy staff, they comfort me." Since I discovered this process, I have a whole new meaning for "Thy staff." And believe me, they *do* comfort me.

How Spirit Talks to You

So, how does Spirit talk to you? You'll know in many ways. Most commonly you'll notice that life just seems to work out, where previously it was difficult. Things start falling into place, seemingly miraculously. Details get ironed out, and monumental tasks come together more smoothly and easily than you could have imagined. Somehow you end up doing just the right thing at just the right time.

You may meet someone who knows the perfect person to do a job for you. You may hear that someone is giving away the very item you were planning to buy. You may impulsively take a detour that leads you to the ideal location for a purpose you have in mind. Or you may be drawn to pick up a greeting card that has the precise answer to a question you've been asking.

Often my answers come in the form of messages from other people. On one occasion, I went to a home-improvement store to buy linoleum tiles for our kitchen floor. On the way, I hired a spiritual interior decorator to help me pick out a design that would go well with our décor while staying within our budget. As I stood looking at the selection, a customer walked by. He leaned over as if to tell me a secret, pointed to one of the tiles, and said, "I put this one in my daughter's kitchen and it looks great." I smiled, knowing I had my answer. And of course it turned out to be the perfect choice. Experiences like this one happen so frequently that I find myself excitedly anticipating how the next message will be delivered.

And I'm not the only one who receives help this way. My friend Judy was in the supermarket one day, looking for a bottle of wine for a friend. All she knew was that he had recently become a fan of Australian red wines. Since she had accidentally left her reading glasses in the car, she couldn't see to read any details on the bottles and had no idea where in the vast aisle to locate something special for him. So she hired a spiritual wine selector and went off to do the rest of her shopping. When she returned a few minutes later, she found a man and a woman carefully studying a bottle of red wine. She asked if they could suggest something good, and the woman replied, "Well, I know nothing about wine, but my sister is a connoisseur and she says this Australian Shiraz is the best there is!" So of course Judy bought a bottle, and it turned out to be her friend's favorite kind.

You'll also find inspiration to be a constant advisor in your life if you open up to it. (Notice that the word *inspiration* contains the word *spirit*.) For instance, in the past I often found myself groping for information to explain what was going on with my clients' health. But since I've started hiring spiritual assistants, I find that all of a sudden a thought just appears. It's a thought *between* my thoughts, one that's not my own. I hear myself saying, "Oh, of course, we need to check this." That's how they talk to me — they bring in the thought, the inspiration. That knowing has just become a part of my life.

Spirit can talk to you in other ways as well, but a lot depends on your particular mode of receiving. Here are the four main types of communication:

- *Clairvoyance:* You actually see pictures or even movies in your mind, or you see auras and information in other people's energy fields.

- *Clairaudience:* You hear a voice (often it sounds like your own) either inside or outside your head.

- *Clairsentience:* You get information via a bodily sensation such as chills or light-headedness.

- *Claircognizance:* You just *know* and often can't explain how. I put my intuition in this category.

Just be open and aware, and listen for what your spiritual workforce is trying to tell you. Discover your mode of receiving inspiration. Pay attention to the synchronicities and seeming coincidences that show up, and then follow their lead. It will begin happening with such frequency that you'll have no doubt Spirit is involved. You'll just know. It's like a friend talking to you. The transmissions will be as clear as day.

CHAPTER 10

How Does It *work?*

When I give talks on Hiring the Heavens, one common question I hear is, "But how does it work?" The idea of employing Spirit — and having it come through according to our asking — seems to fall into the realm of unexplainable phenomena. But far from being some mysterious, airy-fairy concept, this process of asking the Heavens for support calls upon principles as old as the cosmos. The literal interpretation, of course, is that angelic or other benevolent spiritual beings are abundantly available to assist us. But how exactly does it happen? Let's take a look at a couple of possibilities.

The Power of Thought

For those not particularly metaphysically inclined, we might say we're simply harnessing focused intention and thought in a way that the subconscious mind understands. That alone — the power of our mind and our words — has been shown time and again to be consistently effective in creating physical manifestations, emotional states, and inexplicable synchronicities. Our thoughts have more ability to affect our reality than we usually realize. Some would argue that all of creation comes from the power of thought, God's thought.

I would venture to say that simply our *belief* that this will work is reason enough to manifest its glorious possibilities. I've witnessed this phenomenon over and over in my practice. A client's or a practitioner's belief system can be integral in bringing about desired results. In other words, if we believe it will work and look for that confirmation, our intent alone is enough to produce the effects. To me, this is further proof that we are indeed powerful creators.

Universal Law

For those more accustomed to things metaphysical, we might say that we invoke universal law when we ask for assistance from the Universe. Far beyond goal setting, positive thinking, or affirmations, this phenomenon is a natural consequence of a law that applies to us all.

Called the Law of Attraction by some, this principle asserts that the vibration created by our thoughts and feelings sends a magnetized signal out into the Universe and draws its resonant match back to us. The Universe literally launches the objects of our attention our way!

No doubt many of you have read books, listened to tapes, or attended workshops that addressed the Law of Attraction in one form or another. Many teachers have shared this message through the ages. (Think of "As you sow, so shall you reap," "What goes around comes around," and the Golden

Rule.) If you wish to learn more about the subject, you'll have no trouble finding an abundance of sources that explore it in depth. For example, you could check out the inspirational section in a bookstore or type "Law of Attraction" into your favorite internet search engine.

Who Knows? Who Cares?

The truth is I don't think anyone can tell you exactly how this works with absolute certainty. As with so many things in life, there is an element of mystery to this process that we eventually have to accept on faith. But from my point of view, that is immaterial. Whether we know how it works or not, it's a wonderful way to live, one that brings great joy and a masterful sense of creating. Now who doesn't want that? How does it work? Beats me — it just does!

However, I can't promise that the Hiring the Heavens process will work for all of you. No one idea is appropriate or timely for everyone. All I can say is try it. You may not see obvious results right away. But the more you focus your intention, the more you marshal your positive energy, the more likely you'll be to succeed in manifesting the results you want. If you take to it like a duck to water, then fly — or swim — with it. If not, please don't feel there's something wrong with you. There are many doorways into a working relationship with Spirit.

CHAPTER 11

What Will It *cost* Me?

I also encounter a number of questions about cost because the term *hire* implies a payment of some kind. The thought of Hiring the Heavens brings up all sorts of uncertainty about our ability to earn the help we receive, and it reveals some of our commonly held beliefs about deservedness, struggle, and scarcity. I'm here to set your mind at ease. You'll be delighted to learn how the spiritual world gets paid. Let's look at how energy exchange works in the nonphysical dimension.

You Don't Have to Earn It

Here's some good news: You don't have to earn the assistance of your celestial staff. You don't have to spend a certain amount of time in a religious setting, or in devotion or prayer or meditation. Just as you don't have to earn the air you breathe, spiritual help is yours simply because you're alive.

I received a key message when I was inspired to write this book. Your angels *want* to be included in your life. They want you to call upon them. They are eager for you to know that their loving energy is there for you anytime, anywhere, in any situation — however trivial you may think it is. They are never further away than your next thought.

Spiritual Salary?

"But," you may ask, "if I'm hiring this energy, what am I giving in return?" The most wonderful thing about this process is that the payment comes in the only form of currency the spiritual world knows, and that is *love and joy*. Energy exchange in the ether is a vibrational thing, and there's no higher level of vibration than love and joy. This is another win-win situation. The more love and joy you experience, the more you have to give others. And the more love and joy *they* experience, the more *they* have to give. And on and on.

But there's more to the story. Just as you must do something to generate the physical currency of money, you must also do something to generate the spiritual currency of love and joy. And that is . . .

Payment through Presence

You have to wake up and experience life with deeper presence than ever before. To do this requires making a shift in perception that allows you to expand your awareness and take responsibility for who you truly are.

Let's take another look at the final drawing from chapter 6.

Do you grasp the significance of the *Self* as the *o* in *God*? Understand that you are a creator with God and the Spirits of Creation, and that *through you* God experiences and creates. Do you know how important that makes you — how the Universe is counting on *you*? This is the shift in perception that changes everything:

Payment through presence means you're seeing the world the way God — through your eyes — sees it.

This is huge. Stop for a moment and ponder it — but don't be intimidated. Just make a commitment to see yourself as the creator of your world, with full authority to call upon the divine power existing within you and all of the Heavens. See yourself as a creator rather than someone with no choices. And make a decision to cultivate a profound awareness of the perfection in all that surrounds you each day. Choose thoughts and words of gratitude at every opportunity. Become a conscious participant in your life. Spend less time on autopilot and more time in mindful awareness. Notice those moments when you become preoccupied with life's daily grind. Resolve to take a deep breath at such times and remind yourself of who you truly are — *and Who is experiencing your life with you.* This is what is meant by "raising your consciousness," and it is a huge responsibility. You're carrying God with you!

When you embrace this way of being, you generate an energetic flow of love and joy, literally creating those vibrations where they did not exist before. Your smiles and laughter expand throughout all time and space, increasing the joy on Earth as well as in the spiritual realm. *That's* how the spiritual world gets paid, and it's the only payment required. We can all afford that.

Not a Free Ride

Knowing that you have a willing and talented heavenly resource pool to draw upon might give you the impression that all you have to do is sit back and delegate. On the contrary, your first and foremost responsibility is to *create* — and boy, are you going to be busy! Your job is to think of all the wonderful ways you want to enjoy your life, and all the exciting adventures you want to experience. Then get down to business. If you ask the Spirits of Creation for help with a project and then refuse to be involved, nothing gets done. There's plenty you must do. You'll notice, however, that your tasks flow with ease and your work is more like play. You'll be thrilled to find that you can let go of the struggle.

If you're searching for a job, for example, you can hire celestial assistants to help you find the perfect position — but you still have to go for the interviews and perform the work. Remember the story about my spiritual wardrobe consultant? In that case, the clothes didn't just spontaneously appear in my closet. I still had to do the shopping. Likewise with my spiritual book-writing staff: I had to spend hours and hours developing and writing out my ideas. What would have happened if I had refused to pick up a pencil?

Hiring the Heavens doesn't provide a free ride, but it sure makes the ride more fun — and infinitely more creative!

CHAPTER *12*

The Realization of *you*

My hope and intention is that this book will bring you a new perspective on your divine nature and a new awareness of the exhilarating personal relationship you can have with Spirit.

Open the Universal Yellow Pages and begin creating your world anew, with revived enthusiasm. Rediscover forgotten dreams and write an exciting new script for your life. In no time at all you'll be amazed at how your desires and wishes start to manifest with ease. Joyous serendipity will be your constant companion as you let the Universe orchestrate the fulfillment of your dreams.

Ask for assistance in every endeavor, knowing you are bringing joy to your divine helpers just as they bring joy to you. Stay in a receptive mode to fully experience all the fantastic solutions they deliver to your door.

Take the time to develop a close relationship with your celestial teammates by visiting with them frequently. Talk to them just as if they were friends here on Earth. All employees need feedback, need to be praised for their productive efforts — and so do your celestial helpers. Praise them, thank them for the wonderful work they do, and show your appreciation for their loving presence in your life.

Ask for the highest and greatest good for all concerned, letting your heavenly hires arrange the details. Have faith that everything is in divine order. Enjoy the process and remember that your life is a work in progress. Cut out your Angel Express Card — and never leave home without it.

And Then One Day . . .

It will happen. One ordinary day you'll be waking up in the morning, or riding in the car, or sitting down for dinner. All at once you'll be overcome with an incredible sense of awe and joy that will bring tears to your eyes. And you'll finally get it. For at least an instant you'll *know in your heart* the Divine, the God, the Creator that is *you*. And you'll be incredibly honored to be part of this thing we call life. At last you'll feel a connection to Spirit that is undeniable. And you'll recognize the gift you've been given — and the gift that you are.

acknowledgments

Oh my gosh, my book is here!

I wish to thank my editors: Laurie Masters, who helped me get this project off the ground; and Judy Patton, without whose help it never would have landed.

Thanks to the entire staff at New World Library for their dedication to perfecting the manuscript and for their foresight to present this book to the world.

Thanks also to the many friends, clients, and acquaintances who inspired me to write.

And special thanks to my husband, Eric, who has always given me wings to fly.

About the *author*

Jean Slatter is an intuitive natural health practitioner with credentials in nutrition, herbology, and naturopathy. She is also an inspirational speaker and offers workshops, helping others find joy in all facets of life. She lives in northern California with her husband and four children. Visit her website at www.jeanslatter.com.

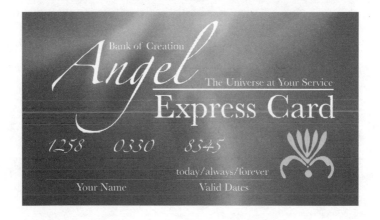

Committee *worksheets*

Committee Worksheet

Name of Your Committee: _____

Mission Statement: _____

_____

Committee Members: _____

_____

_____

Task List: _____

_____

_____

_____

_____

_____

_____

Committee Worksheet

Name of Your Committee: _____

Mission Statement: _____

_____

Committee Members: _____

_____

_____

Task List: _____

_____

_____

_____

_____

_____

_____

Committee Worksheet

Name of Your Committee: _____

Mission Statement: _____

_____

Committee Members: _____

_____

_____

Task List: _____

_____

_____

_____

_____

_____

_____

Committee Worksheet

Name of Your Committee: _____

Mission Statement: _____
_____

Committee Members: _____
_____
_____

Task List: _____
_____
_____
_____
_____
_____
_____

Committee Worksheet

Name of Your Committee: _____

Mission Statement: _____

_____

Committee Members: _____

_____

_____

Task List: _____

_____

_____

_____

_____

_____

_____

Committee Worksheet

Name of Your Committee: _____

Mission Statement: _____
_____

Committee Members: _____
_____
_____

Task List: _____
_____
_____
_____
_____
_____
_____

Committee Worksheet

Name of Your Committee: _____

Mission Statement: _____
_____

Committee Members: _____
_____
_____

Task List: _____
_____
_____
_____
_____
_____
_____
_____

Committee Worksheet

Name of Your Committee:_____

Mission Statement:_____
_____

Committee Members:_____
_____
_____

Task List: _____
_____
_____
_____
_____
_____
_____

Committee Worksheet

Name of Your Committee:_____

Mission Statement:_____

_____

Committee Members: _____

_____

_____

Task List:_____

_____

_____

_____

_____

_____

_____

Committee Worksheet

Name of Your Committee:_____

Mission Statement:_____

_____

Committee Members:_____

_____

_____

Task List:_____

_____

_____

_____

_____

_____

_____

New World Library is dedicated to
publishing books and audio products
that inspire and challenge us to improve
the quality of our lives and our world.

Our products are available
in bookstores everywhere.
For our catalog, please contact:

New World Library
14 Pamaron Way
Novato, California 94949

Phone: (415) 884-2100 or (800) 972-6657
Catalog requests: Ext. 50
Orders: Ext. 52
Fax: (415) 884-2199

E-mail: escort@newworldlibrary.com
Website: www.newworldlibrary.com